NATIONAL GEOGRAPHIC | GLOBAL ISSUES

CLIMATE CHANGE

Andrew J. Milson, Ph.D.
Content Consultant
University of Texas at Arlington

NATIONAL GEOGRAPHIC LEARNING | CENGAGE Learning

Acknowledgments

Grateful acknowledgment is given to the authors, artists, photographers, museums, publishers, and agents for permission to reprint copyrighted material. Every effort has been made to secure the appropriate permission. If any omissions have been made or if corrections are required, please contact the Publisher.

Instructional Consultant: Christopher Johnson, Evanston, Illinois

Teacher Reviewer: Mary Trichel, Atascocita Middle School, Humble, Texas

Photographic Credits

Front Cover, Inside Front Cover, Title Page ©Ralph Lee Hopkins/National Geographic Stock. **4** (bg) ©Ralph Lee Hopkins/National Geographic Stock. **6** (bg) ©Barry Lewis/In Pictures/Corbis. **7** (tl) Precision Graphics. **8** (bg) Mapping Specialists. **10** (bg) ©REUTERS/Daniel Leclair. **11** (bl) Mapping Specialists. **13** (bg) ©Thony Belizaire/AFP/Getty Images/Newscom. (br) ©REUTERS/Goes/noaa RC/MR. **14** (bg) ©parasola/agefotostock. (tl) ©Jose R. Madera/STAFF/El Nuevo Dia/Newscom. **16** (bg) ©Patrick J. Endres/Alamy. **19** (bg) ©Colin Monteath/Hedgehog House/Minden Pictures. (tr) Precision Graphics. **20** (bg) ©ZUMA Press/Newscom. (tl) ©REUTERS/Alister Doyle. **22** (bg) ©Armin Rose/Alamy. (bl) ©Fiona Stewart/Oceans 8 Productions. **24** (t) ©Fiona Stewart/Oceans 8 Productions. (br) ©Ronald Karpilo/Alamy. **27** (t) ©AP Photo/Jennifer Knight. **28** (tr) ©Brand X Pictures/Jupiterimages. **30** (br) ©Reinhard Dirscherl/Wireframe/agefotostock. (tr) ©Thony Belizaire/AFP/Getty Images/Newscom. **31** (bg) ©Don Farrall/Photodisc/Getty Images. (tr) ©Christopher Groenhout/Lonely Planet Images/Getty Images. (br) ©Patrick J. Endres/Alamy. (bl) ©Colin Monteath/Hedgehog House/Minden Pictures.

Print Number: 10 Print Year: 2024
Printed in Mexico

WCN: 01-100-414

Visit National Geographic Learning online at www.NGSP.com.

Visit our corporate website at www.cengage.com.

ISBN: 978-07362-97882

Introducing the ISSUE

Earth's CHANGI CLIMATE

HOW DOES CLIMATE CHANGE AFFECT LIFE ON EARTH?

Polar bears make their homes far from people, in the frozen Arctic region. Using floating sea ice as platforms, they stalk their main prey: seals. However, the polar bears' icy home is changing. The sea ice on which they depend is shrinking. The reason is **climate change**, which is a long-term change in the average weather conditions on Earth. The specific type of climate change is **global warming**, a rise in the average temperature near Earth's surface. Today's climate change affects more than polar bears. It affects all life on Earth.

Arctic sea ice is forming later in the year and melting earlier. As a result, polar bears have a shorter hunting season. If sea ice continues to shrink, two-thirds of polar bears could disappear by 2050.

SIGNS OF CLIMATE CHANGE

Over the past 100 years, Earth's average temperature has risen about 1.4° Fahrenheit. This may not seem like much, but this rise is having global effects. It is changing weather patterns and causing animal habitats to disappear. Polar glaciers and ice sheets in Earth's coldest regions are shrinking.

Although most scientists agree the planet is warming, some people deny it or disagree on *why* it's happening. Earth's climate has changed many times in the past. Is the current climate change part of a natural cycle, as some people claim?

In the United States, almost one-third of greenhouse gas emissions come from transportation vehicles, mostly cars.

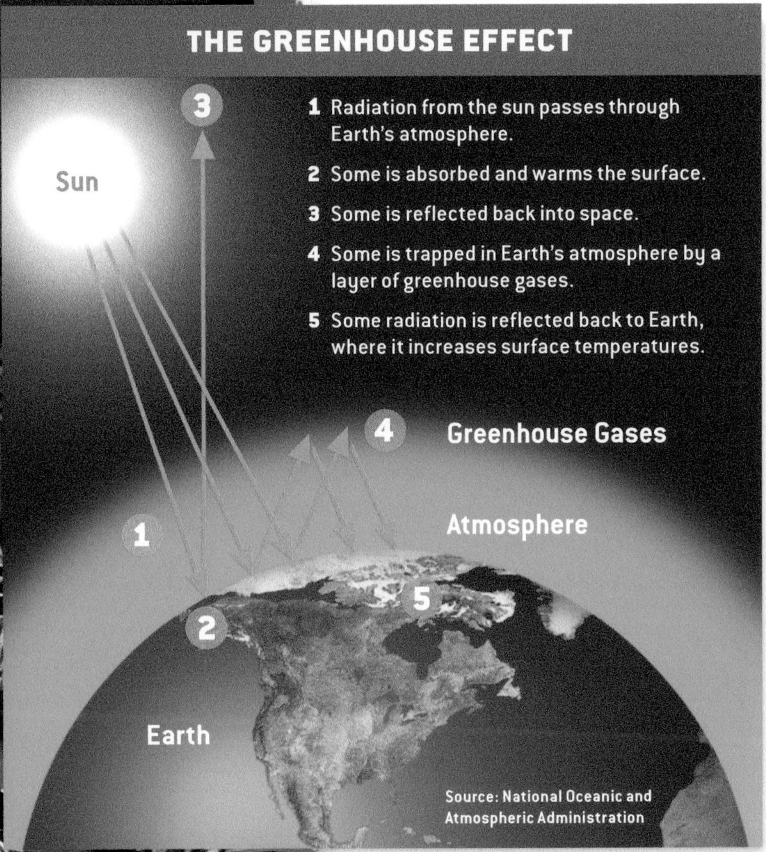

Source: National Oceanic and Atmospheric Administration

WHY IS EARTH WARMING?

Most scientists do not consider current climate change as part of a natural cycle. Instead, they blame global warming on human activities, specifically the burning of **fossil fuels**. Carbon-based fossil fuels, such as coal and oil, form in the earth from decaying plants and animals over millions of years. These fuels power electricity plants, businesses, homes, and vehicles.

As fossil fuels burn, they release chemical compounds called **greenhouse gases** into the atmosphere. There they trap heat near Earth's surface. Greenhouse gases include methane, nitrous oxide, water vapor, and carbon dioxide (CO_2). Burning fossil fuels has increased CO_2 levels by one-third since the mid-1700s.

Scientists want to reduce greenhouse gas levels to no more than twice what they were before the 1800s. To reach this goal, current levels would need to be cut by 50 to 80 percent. Scientists recommend turning to **renewable energy** sources, such as the sun, wind, and water. Unlike fossil fuels, these sources do not harm the environment.

Most scientists believe that global warming is affecting weather patterns around the globe. Many predict even more extreme weather events. Read on to learn about climate change in two very different regions: the Caribbean and Antarctica.

Explore the Issue

1. **Analyze Causes** How do greenhouse gases contribute to global warming?
2. **Analyze Effects** How is global warming affecting Earth's coldest regions?

Climate Challe

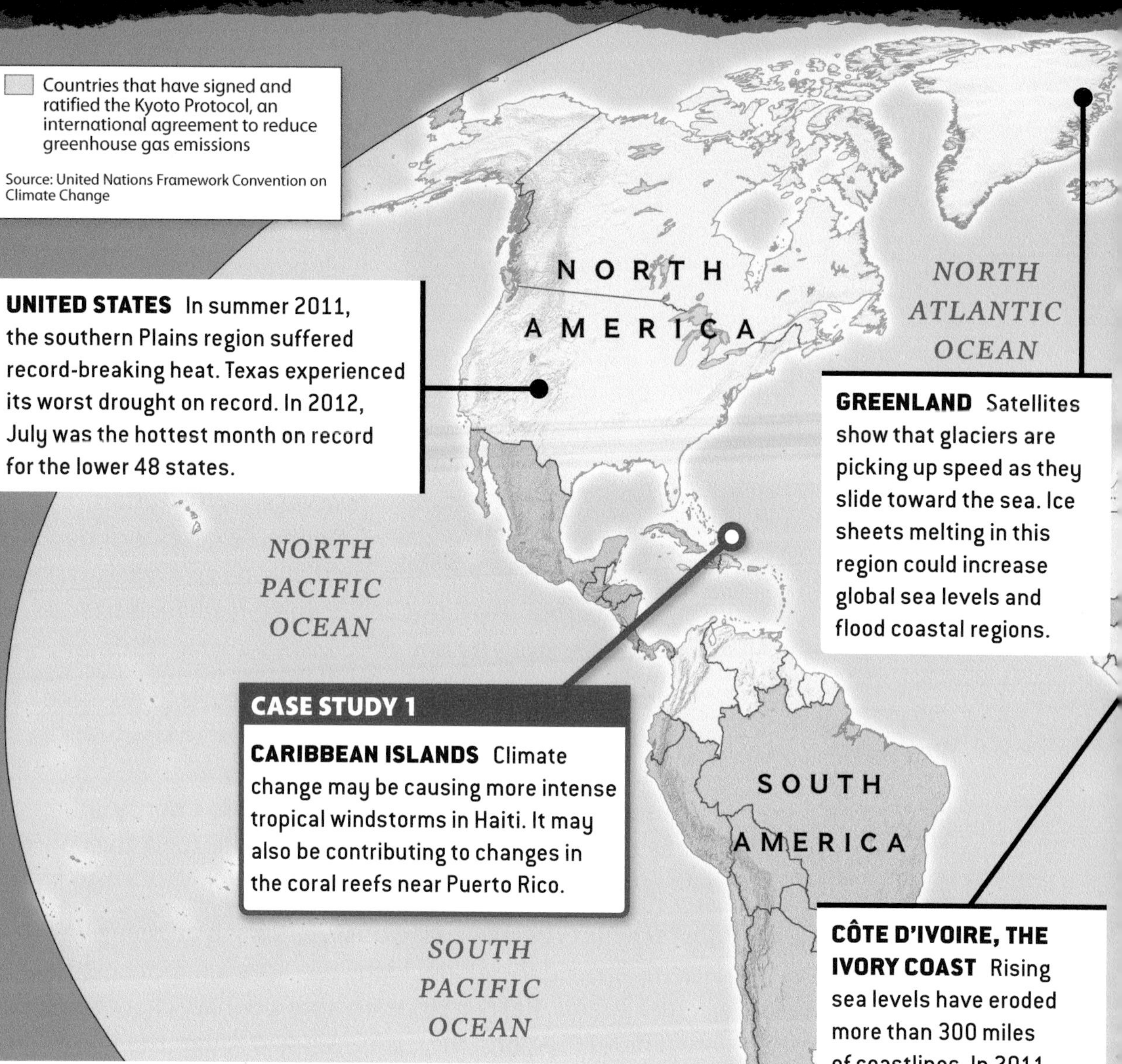

UNITED STATES In summer 2011, the southern Plains region suffered record-breaking heat. Texas experienced its worst drought on record. In 2012, July was the hottest month on record for the lower 48 states.

GREENLAND Satellites show that glaciers are picking up speed as they slide toward the sea. Ice sheets melting in this region could increase global sea levels and flood coastal regions.

CASE STUDY 1

CARIBBEAN ISLANDS Climate change may be causing more intense tropical windstorms in Haiti. It may also be contributing to changes in the coral reefs near Puerto Rico.

CÔTE D'IVOIRE, THE IVORY COAST Rising sea levels have eroded more than 300 miles of coastlines. In 2011, coastal homes in Abidjan were destroyed and several dozen families lost their homes.

Explore the Issue

1. **Interpret Maps** What kinds of extreme weather events were linked to climate change in the United States and Pakistan?
2. **Explain** How might the melting of ice sheets in Greenland affect the coastal regions of Africa?

nges

Study the map and read the callouts to learn more about the effects of climate change around the world.

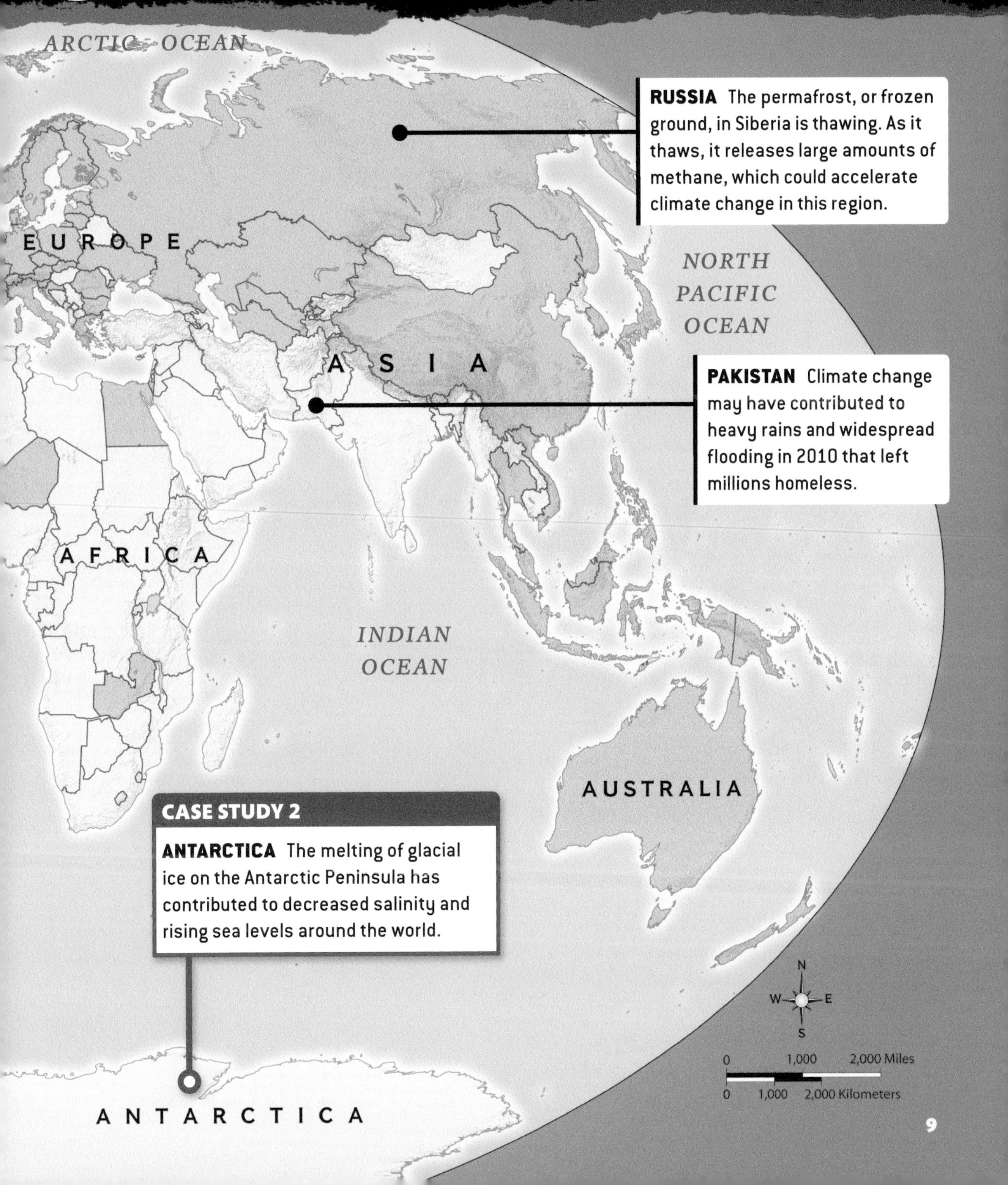

Case Study ONE

Climate Challeng IN THE CARIBBEAN

In 2005, Hurricane Wilma fueled powerful waves that crashed over the sea front and flooded buildings in Havana, Cuba. Extreme tropical storms threaten people and property along Caribbean coastlines every year.

Located between two continents and two oceans, the Caribbean islands lie in the path of hurricanes.

A TROPICAL PARADISE

Most people imagine a tropical paradise when they think of the Caribbean islands. They see rain forests with abundant wildlife, white sand beaches, sparkling ocean waters, and coral reefs with colorful marine life. The Caribbean's natural beauty attracts millions of tourists each year. About 40 million people make their homes on these oceanic islands. Most live in cities along the coasts rather than inland. Many make their living from the sea. Others work in the hotels and restaurants that serve tourists.

While the people depend on the sea, living near the water exposes them to the effects of climate change. The Caribbean islands produce only small amounts of greenhouse gases. Yet global warming threatens the people and their livelihoods.

STORMS BREWING, SEAS RISING

Many scientists believe the Caribbean islands may face more extreme weather events brought on by climate change. Most of the Caribbean islands lie in the path of **hurricanes**, strong tropical windstorms that form at sea. According to weather experts, hurricanes are growing more powerful because of warmer waters in the Atlantic Ocean. Over the past 35 years, the temperature of the ocean's surface water has warmed by 1° Fahrenheit. Warmer waters increase water vapor and precipitation, conditions that produce larger hurricanes.

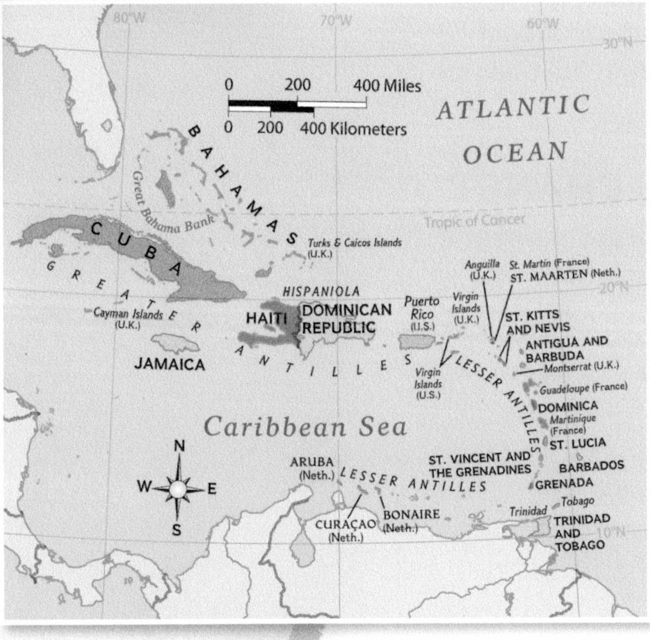

Warmer waters also threaten marine **ecosystems**—the communities of plants and animals that live in the ocean. Many coral reef systems have already declined or died off. A rise in Earth's sea levels is also occurring, partly because warm water expands as it grows warmer. As global warming melts glaciers and ice sheets in Earth's coldest regions, rising sea levels will erode shorelines and flood cities along coastlines. Millions of people could be forced to relocate. Two locations in the Caribbean—Haiti and Puerto Rico—already show dramatic effects of climate change.

HAITI BATTLES HURRICANES

Haiti (HEY-tee) sits on the western edge of the island of Hispaniola (his-puhn-YOH-luh). The island is right in the alley of powerful hurricanes. In 2008, a Haitian fisherman named Garvins Novembre (noh-VAHNBR) lived in a hut on a beach. As Hurricane Gustav hit the Haitian coast, floodwaters poured down the hillsides. Novembre realized that he and his baby daughter might not survive. Acting quickly, he fled with his daughter in a small boat. They escaped with their lives.

Novembre was lucky. Four major storms that year left 1,100 people dead or missing. Crops and homes were destroyed, and many children died of malnutrition. That year, hurricanes caused more than one billion dollars in damage. Since 2000, Haiti has been the victim of increasingly powerful hurricanes that have devastated the country.

The problem is that warmer waters generate more energy, making hurricanes more destructive. Flooding has also been a problem. During the 2008 storm, people with small homes along the coast had to flee to escape huge waves that washed away buildings.

Other environmental problems in Haiti have worsened the impact of the storms. For example, about 98 percent of the country's forests have been cut. The resulting **deforestation**—the loss of forests due to clearing of trees—has made flooding worse. This is because tree roots act like sponges to soak up and hold water. When the trees are gone, water can run freely down hillsides.

GRAPPLING WITH CLIMATE CHANGE

To lessen the impact of flooding events, the government of Haiti has taken steps to restore the environment. In 2006, it created a plan of action to address climate change.

One initiative is reforestation, or the planting of trees. Helped by international organizations, Haiti's farmers now plant mango and avocado trees on hillsides near their homes to prevent soil erosion and stabilize the soil. Trees also give off beneficial oxygen and absorb carbon dioxide, reducing the amount of the greenhouse gas in the atmosphere.

People wade through flooded streets in Port-au-Prince, Haiti. Many businesses and homes were destroyed by Hurricane Tomas in 2010.

In 2004, Hurricane Frances is tracked by a weather satellite over Haiti as it approaches the Bahamas.

In San Juan, Puerto Rico, an efficient mass transit rail system links the capital with other cities and helps reduce pollution from automobiles.

Acting to preserve its unique natural resources, Puerto Rico is taking initiatives to lessen the effects of climate change.

PUERTO RICO: LOSING CORAL REEFS

The island of Puerto Rico is only 352 nautical miles from Haiti, but it is different from Haiti in many ways. The island, which is a territory of the United States, has more roads, bridges, and other public works than Haiti and other neighbors.

Even so, the island is still vulnerable to climate change, especially to rising sea levels. Half of Puerto Rico's population lives in the coastal capital of San Juan (san-WAHN), which lies close to sea level. Even those who do not live near the sea face problems. More and more people have built homes on higher ground where trees once grew. Now, heavy rains and storms cause landslides, just as in Haiti.

Another effect of climate change is the loss of coral reefs, which are underwater structures formed by small marine animals. The reefs form the habitat for thousands of fish and other ocean life. In 2005, scientists discovered that warmer ocean waters were causing widespread **coral bleaching**. Changes in the reef's ecosystem have caused corals to turn white as they lose the colorful algae in their tissues. Scientists estimate that as much as 90 percent of Puerto Rico's coral reefs are dead or dying.

SEEKING CLIMATE SOLUTIONS

Puerto Rico is finding ways to address climate change. In 2011, for example, a healthy coral reef was discovered. The island's Coastal Zone Management Program will develop measures to protect the reef's health.

The island also wants to decrease its use of fossil fuels and explore renewable energy sources, such as building power plants fueled by waste. It has also built a rail system to reduce exhaust pollution from cars. Like Haiti, the island of Puerto Rico is taking initiatives to lessen the effects of climate change.

Explore the Issue

1. **Analyze Problems** How has climate change affected Haiti and Puerto Rico?
2. **Analyze Solutions** How are Haiti and Puerto Rico addressing climate change?

ANTARCTIC Shrinking Ice

Penguin colonies in Antarctica have been declining in numbers. Global warming is affecting their breeding and hunting grounds.

PENGUINS' ICY HOME

Like the polar bears of the Arctic, emperor penguins have an icy home. These hardy birds live in an extreme habitat—frigid Antarctica. They use their wings to swim through water, not fly through the air. Seals and whales, as well as more than 40 species of birds, also spend at least part of their lives in Antarctica. Many return each summer to the ocean that surrounds the continent.

About 98 percent of Antarctica is covered by ice sheets. This layer of glacial ice is more than a mile thick. A surprising variety of wildlife adapt to this icy region. However, no native people live here, as they do in the Arctic region. Scientists, explorers, and tourists only visit the continent. Despite the scarcity of people, the effects of climate change have reached even this remote continent. The evidence lies in what is happening to the gigantic glaciers of Antarctica.

MELTING GIANTS

The impact of climate change on Antarctica started to become clear in January 2002. Scientists were checking satellite photographs of West Antarctica, and they saw something strange. An **ice shelf**, a thick platform of ice that extends from the shore into the ocean, had developed large cracks in its surface. The area, known as the Larsen Ice Shelf, was about 1,250 square miles in size, almost as big as the state of Rhode Island.

In February, several gigantic icebergs broke off from the ice shelf. By March, Larsen broke apart completely into icebergs and slush. Scientists blamed the sudden disintegration on warm air and water temperatures.

Between 2002 and April 2009, West Antarctica experienced multiple events in which large ice shelves collapsed into icebergs. The average temperatures of the ocean surrounding Antarctica have warmed by more than 5 degrees. In addition, the air temperature over West Antarctica has warmed slightly by about 1° Fahrenheit since 1957. As a result, glaciers are melting faster than new snowfall can build them.

The breakup of West Antarctica's ice shelves is a sign to scientists that Earth's average temperatures are rising. This phenomenon is affecting the most remote parts of the globe.

A DRAMATIC COLLISION

Meanwhile in East Antarctica, changes have occurred in the Mertz Glacier. In the 1990s, large cracks began to appear in the glacier's massive ice tongue which stuck out from the coastline over the water. In 2010, a 60-mile-long iceberg rammed into the shelf and tore it off the glacier. Although scientists agree the dramatic collision was not caused by global warming, it provided the opportunity to monitor the level, temperature, and saltiness of the ocean.

Scientists have learned that as glacial ice melts, large amounts of freshwater are added to the ocean. This is because glaciers are formed over thousands of years by layers of accumulated snowfall. When massive chunks of glacial ice break away and form icebergs in a process called **calving**, sea levels rise and water temperature drops. In addition, seawater becomes less salty.

Scientists are also measuring the amount of carbon dioxide stored by the ocean water. Similar to trees, Earth's oceans absorb carbon dioxide, which helps slow global warming. At the same time, though, the carbon makes the ocean more acidic. The increase in acidity harms nutrient-rich ocean plants and small sea creatures that feed whales, seals, and penguins.

DEADLY DISRUPTIONS

Large marine animals depend on a diet of nutrient-rich food, such as krill, tiny shrimplike creatures, and plankton, floating organisms that drift in ocean currents. The more acidic ocean waters around the continent have led to an annual decline in these essential food sources.

Disruptions in the underwater food chain have already affected the land animals that make Antarctica their home. Emperor penguin populations, for example, have fallen 50 percent over the past 50 years. What happens in one ocean affects all oceans, and decline or death in one region's ecosystem affects others. According to Will Howard, an Australian scientist, entire ecosystems are at risk. Scientists will continue to study climate events in Antarctica in order to improve their understanding of how changes on the coldest continent will affect all life on Earth.

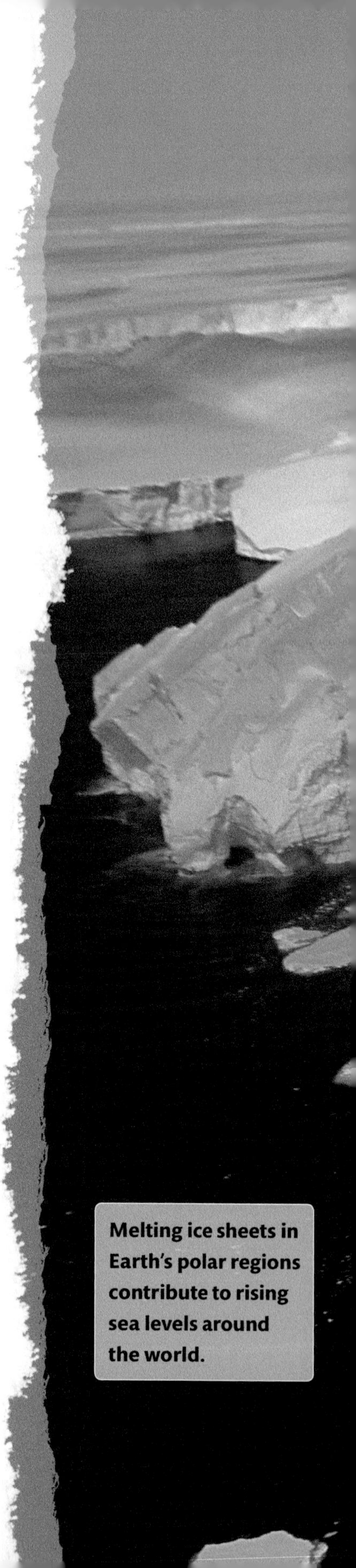

Melting ice sheets in Earth's polar regions contribute to rising sea levels around the world.

HOW ICE CALVES

- Heat from the sun warms the surface of land ice.
- Meltwater deepens cracks and fissures in the ice.
- Rising tides erode and weaken the ice from below.
- Massive ice chunks break off and form icebergs. This process is called calving.

Source: U.S. Geological Survey; Science.howstuffworks.com

A Norwegian researcher uses a snowmobile to collect climate data at Troll Research Station.

A scientist monitors changes in temperature, precipitation, and air quality on the Antarctic Peninsula.

CONDUCTING RESEARCH ON ANTARCTICA

It seems odd that evidence of global warming is not showing up in East Antarctica, which makes up most of the continent. Upon closer examination, however, scientists think one environmental problem may actually mask another.

The reason East Antarctica is not showing the effects of climate change is related to Earth's upper atmosphere, which has a region called the **ozone layer**. This protective layer blocks harmful rays of sun from reaching Earth's surface. However, the layer above the South Pole has a hole in it, caused by chemicals that have been released from spray cans and older air conditioners. This hole actually may have kept East Antarctica's temperature from rising.

Since the use of these harmful chemicals has been banned, the layer has been repairing itself. Now scientists predict a gradual rise in the region's temperature of 3° Celsius by 2100. This will not be enough to melt the continent's main ice sheets. However, some scientists expect melting glaciers to raise sea levels more than 4 feet over the next 100 years.

More than two dozen countries operate research stations along Antarctica's coasts. International treaties encourage countries to work together to preserve the continent's natural resources. Because Antarctica does not have industry or large human populations, it produces low levels of greenhouse gas emissions. Even so, scientists want to limit current levels. Two countries, New Zealand and the United States, are already working together to build wind turbines on Ross Island. The turbines will utilize renewable energy instead of fossil fuels to power the research stations.

As research in this region reveals, Earth's climate system is complex and connected. Changes in Antarctica affect regions thousands of miles away.

Explore the Issue

1. **Explain** Why are oceans becoming more acidic?
2. **Draw Conclusions** How do melting glaciers in Antarctica affect the planet?

NATIONAL GEOGRAPHIC **AT WORK**

Exploring Antarctic Ocean

Under sail to King George Island, Antarctica, explorer Jon Bowermaster crosses Drake Passage, one of the windiest places on Earth.

Towering icebergs rise above the ocean waters near the Antarctic Peninsula.

TAKING EARTH'S PULSE

Explorer Jon Bowermaster has seen the effects of climate change all over the world. Awarded grants by the National Geographic Expeditions Council, he developed the Oceans 8 project. Since 1999, he has explored the oceans of the world and shared his work in documentary films and in articles in magazines such as *National Geographic.*

Bowermaster has led expeditions to all seven continents to study the oceans that surround them. The oceans actually form one vast sea with different names in different places. Covering more than 70 percent of Earth's surface area, the oceans absorb more than 80 percent of the heat trapped by greenhouse gas emissions. Almost half the world's population depends on the oceans for food, transportation, and energy. Rising sea levels threaten billions of people.

CHECKING EARTH'S HEALTH

Explorations to Antarctica, the southernmost continent, are limited by its extreme climate. During the long Antarctic winter, ice doubles the surface area of the continent. This natural expansion provides a suitable habitat for penguins, seals, and seabirds but not for people. Thick ice sheets cover the continent year-round. Explorers must wait for the short summer months before they can navigate the waters around Antarctica.

In January 2008, Bowermaster and his team set sail for West Antarctica. Just like the penguins that live in the region, the explorers quickly learned to recognize ice that was unstable and dangerous. When floating chunks of ice collide, even large ships with strong thick hulls can become trapped in ice jams that suddenly form. The team decided to launch kayaks from the transport ship and paddle toward the peninsula. The plan required nerves of steel because floating ice can easily capsize lighter craft.

As the Oceans 8 explorers studied Antarctica's ocean, they found evidence of climate change. Bowermaster says, "If you believe as I do that Earth is a living thing, then Antarctica is its pulse," As explained in Case Study Two, studying climate change in this remote region reveals the health of the whole planet.

In light, maneuverable kayaks, Oceans 8 explorers paddle around floating icebergs off the Fish Islands, Antarctica.

STUDYING THE WATERS

Bowermaster believes that the waters around Antarctica are an important indicator of climate change. These waters contain only about 5 percent of the world's seawater, but they provide a home for nearly 20 percent of its sea life. However, rising temperatures are changing the patterns of the waters' wildlife. For example, Bowermaster noted a decline in the number of Adélie penguins and ocean krill, tiny shrimplike crustaceans that feed larger marine animals, including whales. He also noted an increase in plant populations.

Despite being so far from human populations, the team observed over a dozen tourist ships in the area. Bowermaster commented that not long ago seeing one private sailboat in the area would have been noteworthy. Climate scientists will continue to monitor the effects of tourism on the region.

These photos of Muir Glacier in Alaska were taken 100 years apart. They show the effects of global warming in another part of the world.

KEEPING WATCH

On the expedition, Bowermaster was surprised by the amount and thickness of the ice sheet. These conditions were a result of the previous winter, when Antarctica had colder than usual temperatures. Bowermaster fears that this fact may cause people to question whether climate change in Antarctica is really happening. However, he points out that the ice is due to seasonal weather and is not a sign that climate change isn't real.

Bowermaster learned on his trip that the continent needs to be watched closely. As he says: "If Antarctica is the beating heart of the planet, as I believe it is, it deserves to be cared for with all of our best intentions."

Explore the Issue

1. **Explain** According to Bowermaster, why is it important to keep a close watch on Antarctica's climate?
2. **Draw Conclusions** Why should climate change in Antarctica matter to the rest of the world?

What Can I DO?

Plant a Tree

—and report your results

You don't have to explore the oceans to fight climate change. You might start by reducing your use of fossil fuel energy. Trees help reduce the amount of carbon dioxide in the atmosphere. By planting trees in your community, you can make a difference.

IDENTIFY

- Find out about tree-planting projects in your school or community.
- Invite experts to explain the best kinds of native trees for your climate. Also learn when and how to plant saplings.
- Find a donor source for trees. Arrange for their delivery.

ORGANIZE

- Advertise your project through school or local media.
- Have volunteers sign up to plant the trees and gather supplies, such as gloves, shovels, water, and mulch, for planting day.
- Schedule volunteers to water the newly planted trees weekly.

Students work together to plant a tree in their community on Arbor Day.

DOCUMENT

- Take before-and-after photos of the site(s) where you plant the trees and photograph the trees during each season.
- Label your trees with signs or make a map of the area that shows the kinds of trees you have planted.
- Keep a log about when and how you care for the trees, and record their growth each month.

SHARE

- Use your photos and recordings to create a multimedia presentation about your tree-planting project and share it with your class.
- Create a blog about your project from planning to planting and follow-up. Include information about trees and climate change.
- Encourage others to plant trees by creating a visual display of your project for your local library or community center.

Research &
WRITE
Narrative

Write a Narrative

Climate change has already caused dramatic changes over recent decades. Melting ice and snow in Glacier National Park and the Alps, bleaching of coral reefs, and drought in parts of Africa are just a few examples. Your task is to choose a place to research a dramatic event related to climate change. Your purpose is to use your findings to plan and write a narrative.

RESEARCH

Use the Internet, books, and articles to find the following information:

- What was the climate like in the early 1900s?
- How has the climate changed over time?
- What dramatic natural events occurred, and how are they related to climate change?

As you research, be sure to take notes and keep track of your sources.

DRAFT

Review your notes about the location you chose. Then select one climate event to dramatize in your story.

- Begin by describing the event's setting with vivid details that will engage the reader.
- Narrate the story through the eyes of a person or an animal. Establish and maintain a consistent point of view, and provide the context for your story.
- The middle paragraphs should present the sequence of events that led to the changes. Use precise words and sensory language to describe them. Use helpful transitions to convey sequence.
- In the final paragraph, wrap up the story in a way that makes the reader want to learn more.

REVISE & EDIT

Read your first draft to make sure that it clearly tells the story of how climate change affected one place in time.

- Does the beginning get the attention of your audience and introduce the topic and setting?
- Does the body of the story present a logical sequence of events and include descriptive details?
- Does the ending flow from the story in a reflective, thought-provoking way?

Revise the narrative to make sure it is clear and complete. Then check your paper for errors in grammar, spelling, and punctuation.

PUBLISH & PRESENT

Now you are ready to publish and present your narrative. Print out your narrative, or write a clean copy by hand. Consider adding photos or graphics to enhance the text. Publish your narrative in a class magazine or Web site.

Visual GLOSSARY

calving *v.*, the process in which massive chunks of glacial ice break away from land and form icebergs

climate change *n.*, a long-term change in average weather conditions on Earth

coral bleaching *n.*, a condition that causes corals to turn white as they lose the colorful algae in their tissues

deforestation *n.*, the process of cutting and clearing trees for fuel or farmland

ecosystem *n.*, a community of living things and their environment

fossil fuel *n.*, a carbon-based energy source formed in the earth

global warming *n.*, a rise in the average temperature near Earth's surface

greenhouse gas *n.*, a chemical compound released into the atmosphere where it traps heat near Earth's surface

hurricane *n.*, a strong tropical storm that forms at sea and often drives high winds and heavy rain inland

ice shelf *n.*, a thick platform of ice that extends from the shore into the ocean

ozone layer *n.*, a layer of the upper atmosphere that blocks harmful rays of the sun

renewable energy *n.*, a natural power source that does not harm the environment

climate change

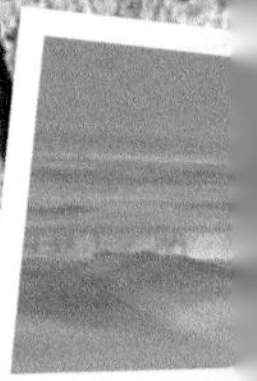

coral bleaching

renewable energy

ecosystem

ice shelf

INDEX

SKILLS